1

2

Keep

Me Safe,

O God.

By

John C Burt

4

Photographs Courtesy of :

davide -cantelli.

marc - olivier - jodoin.

jake - blucker.

tony - eight - media.

abigail - keenan.

pete - willis.

raychan .

Free Downloads on :

unsplash.com

6

7

10

11

12

13

16

17

FOREWORD :

As I write this I have a friend battling cancer and in many ways my reflections upon Psalm 16 come out of my own struggles to pray

20

for him. One morning I got up early to pray for him and just happened upon Psalm 16; which seemed to help me to focus my own prayers for him that morning? I find this Psalm, Psalm 16 to be an encouragement ?

21

The Psalm itself would seem to come out of a period of time when David was feeling oppressed and in real need of the Lord God's help and support? David cries out to the Lord God and

22

also reminds Him of what he has done in his life and what He is like; His Character.

In many ways, the Psalm itself has a rhythm and a sway all its own. It bumps and grinds through it's

23

verses, words and various thoughts and themes. Yet, the main thought always remains the main thought and theme and that is that everything that the Psalmist David has comes from the Lord God

24

and that He , the
Lord God Almighty
is a Good God.
    I found the
Psalm, Psalm 16 to
be incredibly
helpful and my
prayer would be
that you do as
well, as we reflect
upon it.

32

33

34

35

37

1.

From this chapter forwards we want to cite the Word of God, the Psalm , Psalm 16.

40

There will be four different versions of the text given. They will be the ESV, the NIV, the MSG and finally the GNT versions of the text of Psalm 16.

{ ESV }

Psalm 16 : A Psalm of David :

You Will Not Abandon My Soul :

" (1) Preserve me, O God, for in you I

42

take refuge.

(2) I say to
the Lord, " You are my
LORD; I have no good
apart from you."

(3) As for the
saints in the land, they
are the excellent ones,
in whom is all my
delight.

(4) The
sorrows of those who

run after another god shall multiply; their drink offerings of blood I will not pour out or take their names on my lips.

(5) The LORD is my chosen portion and my cup; you hold my lot.

(6) The lines have fallen for me

44

in pleasant places;
Indeed, I have a
beautiful inheritance.
    (7) I will
bless the LORD who
gives me counsel; in
the night also my heart
instructs me.
    (8) I have
set the LORD always
before me; because he
is at my right hand, I

shall not be shaken.
(9) Therefore my heart is glad, and my whole being rejoices; my flesh also dwells secure.
(10) For you will not abandon my soul to Sheol, or let your holy one see corruption.

46

(11) You make known to me the path of life; in your presence there is fullness of joy; at your right hand are pleasures forevermore."

2.

{ N1V }

Psalm 16 : A
Psalm of David:

A miktam of David :

" (1) Keep me safe, my God, for in you I take refuge.
(2) I say to the LORD, " You are my LORD; apart from you I have no good thing."
(3) I say of the holy people who are in the land, " They are

57

the noble ones in whom is all my delight."

(4) Those who run after other gods will suffer more and more.

I will not pour out libations of blood to such gods or take up their names on my lips.

(5) LORD, you alone are my portion and my cup; you make my lot secure.

(6) The boundary lines have fallen for me in pleasant places; surely I have a delightful inheritance.

(7) I will praise the LORD, who

counsels me; even at night my heart instructs me.

(8) I keep my eyes always on the LORD. With him at my right hand, I will not be shaken.

(9) Therefore my heart is glad and my tongue rejoices; my body also will ...

rest secure,

(10) because you will not abandon me to the realm of the dead, nor will you let your faithful one see decay.

(11) You make known to me the path of life; you will fill me with joy in your presence, with eternal

pleasures at your right hand."

64

65

66

67

3.

{ MSG }

Psalm 16 : A
Psalm of David :

A David Song :

" (1 – 2) Keep me
safe, O GOD, I've run for
dear life to you.
        I say to GOD,
" Be my LORD !"
        Without you, nothing
makes sense.
        (3) And these
God – chosen lives all
around – what splendid

73

friends they make!

(4) Don't just go shopping for a god. Gods are not for sale.

I swear I'll never treat god - names like brand - names.

(5 - 6) My choice is you, GOD, first and only.

And now I find I'm your choice !

74

You set me up
with a house and yard.
And then you
made me your heir!
(7 - 8) The
wise counsel God gives
when I'm awake is
confirmed by my
sleeping heart.
Day and night I'll
stick with GOD;
I've got a good thing

going and I'm not
letting go.
          (9 – 10) I'm
happy from the inside
out, and from the
outside in,
          I'm firmly
formed.
          You canceled
my ticket to hell –
          that's not my
destination !
76

(11) Now
you've got my feet on
the life path,
        all radiant
from the shining of
your face.
        Ever since you
took my hand,
        I'm on the
right way."

84

86

87

88

89

4.

{ GNT }

Psalm 16 : A
Psalm of David:

A Prayer of Confidence:

" (1) Protect me, O GOD; I trust in you for safety.
(2) I say to the LORD, " You are my LORD; all the good things I have come from you."
(3) How

excellent are the LORD's faithful people! My greatest pleasure is to be with them.

(4) Those who rush to other gods bring many troubles on themselves.

I will not take part in their sacrifices; I will not

worship their gods.

(5) You, LORD, are all 1 have, and you give me all 1 need; my future is in your hands.

(6) How wonderful are your gifts to me; how good they are!

(7) 1 praise the LORD, because he

guides me,
and in the
night my conscience
warns me.
(8) 1 am
always aware of the
LORD's presence; he is
near, and nothing can
shake me.
(9) And so 1
am thankful and glad,
and 1 feel completely
94

secure,

(10) because
you protect me from
the power of death.

I have served
you faithfully,

and you will not
abandon me to the
world of the dead.

(11) You will
show me the path that
leads to life;

your presence fills
me with joy
and brings me
pleasure forever."

96

5.

We will start by considering verses 1 and 2 of Psalm 16?

114

We will be considering the Psalm in lots of two verses at a time. In the end, the Psalm is a cry from the heart !

115

(ESV)
" (1) Preserve me, O GOD, for in you I take refuge.

(2) I say to the LORD,

116

"You are my
LORD;
I have no
good apart
from you."

Verse one is
really very much a
cry from the very
heart of David , the
Psalmist in a real

117

way. It would seem David at this point in the Psalm fears for his very life and in the end recognizes that it is the Lord God Almighty he needs to have his trust in; it is He who is his refuge in trouble?

The idea or notion of the Lord God Almighty being a refuge or sanctuary for His people and the individual is one that accords well with the rest of the Word of God. It is very much an idea or notion or concept that is prevalent in the writings of the Psalter and the wider Old Testament itself. In the end, it was in the Lord God Almighty that the people of the Lord God Almighty could find a place of both refuge and sanctuary. Right from the start , the people of the Lord God Almighty; His chosen people, His Treasure and His Possession had to fight for their very existence. They had always needed a place of refuge; which they found in the Lord God Almighty Himself. This is the way that the Lord God Almighty had designed things, the very way and ways He wanted His people to come to Him and to find their refuge and their very real security in His very Presence.

In some ways; one could read verse two as a statement or restatement of belief or faith in the Lord God Almighty by David himself?

123

In this verse, David would once again seem to be saying and affirming that the Lord God Almighty is indeed his God....'You are my LORD?' But he also takes this further and affirms as well that all the great and good things in his very life come from the very hand of the Lord God Almighty. He sees that there is no good apart from that which comes from the Lord God Almighty? To a ...

degree, he is affirming in this part of the verse the very goodness of the Lord God Almighty. He is in reality affirming through these very words the character of the Lord God Almighty as being a God who is at His heart Good and has Goodness as His main value. David has come to see that in the end, there is no form or forms of goodness that do not in reality come from the Lord God Almighty ?

127

In some ways, one could see the opening two verses as being like a sketch diagram or picture of the Lord God Almighty and the relationship that David has with Him? David cries out to the Lord God Almighty, because he knows he can trust Him and His Goodness and His very Character and desires for he, himself? David is setting the very groundwork for the rest of the ....

Psalm, Psalm 16; he is making a very clear statement as to who he is addressing his song, his pleas and his very words of prayer to; the Lord God Almighty who is a Lord God Almighty who is ...

130

always Good. David has seen this to be true of the very workings of the Lord God Almighty in and through His workings in his own life and times. He knows , who he knows and has faith, belief and trust in?

138

139

142

143

6.

Within this chapter we will be considering verses 3 and 146

4 and what they have to say to us all? In these verses David the Psalmist says some things which are significant!

(ESV)

" (3) As for the saints in the land, they are the excellent ones, in whom is all my delight.

(4) The sorrows of those who run after another god shall multiply; their drink offerings of

blood I will
not pour out
or take their
names on my
lips."

It is worth
noting that David
does not talk
about all the very
150

people of the Lord God Almighty; he rather addresses himself to the saints in the land. All of which would mean that there were still people who were faithful people to the Lord God Almighty ?

David himself takes delight in these 'excellent people' as he calls them being in the land. He would have numbered himself amongst those people he called the ' saints' of the Lord God Almighty? At this point it is worth remembering that David himself was considered by the Lord God Almighty 'to be a man after His own heart.' He understands and knows well the ways of the Lord God Almighty and here he is lauding some of the people of the Lord God Almighty for in reality being faithful and true 'saints' of the Lord God Almighty. The point , I want to make is that, the very real humility of David comes ...

154

through to us in all of this. David was a man used mightily by the Lord God Almighty and yet, he was also a man who was humble and had humility before the Lord God Almighty and the very people of the Lord God Almighty. It might well be that this was caught up in the reasons why David was both a man after the heart of the Lord God Almighty and much used by Him as well.

156

The people who follow after other gods are held in sharp contrast to the 'saints' of the land who follow faithfully the Lord God Almighty? It is all caught up with a concept in terms of the Psalter and in terms of Hebrew Poetry called Parallelism ...You put things that you want to contrast and highlight against each other in close proximity; as here after each other in the very verses of the Psalm? Because of this David's views about those who follow after and pursue other gods other than the Lord God Almighty is in and cannot be in any doubt; it's very plain for all to see from these verses.

   The outcomes of those who follow

other gods rather than the Lord God Almighty, is also contrasted with David's own experiences of the Lord God Almighty in and through his own life and times. All of which makes and emphasizes the very real contrast being made between the other gods that some people follow after and the Lord God Almighty Himself? David himself is very clear that he will not follow both after these other gods or god and also he will not take part in any ceremonies associated with their worship by those who follow them. So, at this juncture in the Psalm , Psalm 16,

162

we have a very clear statement of the reality that David himself would never follow after another god or gods as some people have done in the land? In some ways,

here at this point
in the Psalm, Psalm
16 , we are being
given a picture of
what life was like
in the both the
land and amongst
the very people of
the Lord God
Almighty. Foreign
gods and a god
were always things

which took the people of the Land and the Lord God Almighty away from truly being a people of Himself. It is in many ways like the picture of the world - at - large we have at present and the Lord God Almighty?

168

169

176

177

178

179

7.

In this chapter we will be giving consideration to verses 5 ...

and 6 of
Psalm 16.
The Psalmist
David again
in them
focuses upon
the Lord God
Almighty !

(ESV)

"(5) The LORD is my chosen portion and my cup; you hold my lot. (6) The lines have fallen for me in pleasant places; indeed, I have a beautiful inheritance."

Here in these verses David once again comes back to focusing upon the Lord God Almighty ... In many ways, it is a very clear statement of faith from David .. This is the Lord God Almighty I believe in and here's why I believe in Him? For David, and for ourselves if we are found in the Lord Jesus Christ, then all we have is founded in and upon Him. For David there is nothing outside of the Lord God Almighty's provision in his own life. All things he has come from and through the Lord God Almighty. This is the way we need in our days and in our times to see

186

everything in our lives; we need to see them as being provided by the Lord Jesus Christ, the Father and the Holy Spirit, the Godhead. This is a very real and valid application of the verses of this Psalm; Psalm 16 to ourselves and our lives before the very gaze of the Lord Jesus Christ. To some degree, if we saw everything in our lives as coming from the Lord Jesus Christ, then, things in our own lives would be more stable and more together in Him. It's a place of the beginning of being thankful and having gratitude to the Lord Jesus Christ, the Father and the Holy Spirit, the Godhead, for all they have done.

Verse 6 takes the ideas of verse 5 further; not only does everything come from the Lord God Almighty but in Him David has an inheritance. There is a hope; just a hint of a hope for the future and a future with the Lord God Almighty in it. Also , there is a sense of the blessings of the future with the Lord God Almighty have become a reality in the here and now ... Lines ..

191

or boundary lines would seem to denote property lines and it's markings or boundaries. Whatever it is, they have fallen in pleasant places for David .. He is blessed by the ....

Lord God Almighty. It is not only that he is blessed but that he in reality knows that he has been blessed by the Lord God Almighty Himself.

The words 'beautiful inheritance' are worth noting; they

denote a hope for the future and future blessings from the Lord God Almighty as well. These very words are very much pregnant with real hope and expectation on the part of David that

he does in reality
possess an
inheritance in the
Lord God Almighty.

Given the
times it was written
in and the very
reality that the
people of the Lord
God Almighty had

already been blessed with the Promised Land; David was thinking of more blessings in terms of land as the inheritance from the Lord God Almighty. It is worth noting that the very provision of land was associated with material blessing from the Lord God Almighty. One can see this in the life of the Patriarch Abraham and how he had much wealth , property and therefore blessing from the Lord God Almighty.

It might also be possible to see the ' beautiful inheritance ' that David is talking about as eternal life with the Lord God Almighty? This reflection upon these words of David would seem to fit with the words and the language of later in the Psalm. This hope of an eternity with the Lord God Almighty was present and yet still muted to a degree.

199

While this
hope of an eternity
with the Lord God
Almighty is muted ,
it is still present
and vocalized by
David. Therefore,
one has to wonder
how reflective it is
of the hope of the
everyday people

200

for the hope of an eternity with the Lord God Almighty? It's muted in it's nature when it is viewed against the full blown nature of the hope of an eternity with the Lord God in the New Testament.

202

203

204

205

206

207

208

209

210

211

8.

Within this
chapter we
will give
consideration
216

to verses 7 and 8 and what they have to say to us all? All about the praise of the Lord God Almighty !

(ESV)
" (7) I
bless the
LORD who
gives me
counsel; in
the night also
my heart ...

218

instructs me.
     (8) I have set the LORD always before me; because he is at my right hand, I shall not be shaken."

Here in
verse 7; David
chooses to use the
word bless, the
first time he uses
this word in the
Psalm , although
he has alluded to it
before. David had

much to bless the Lord God Almighty for? If any man was blessed by the Lord God Almighty it was most certainly David; taken as a shepherd boy to the very courts of the King of Israel and ultimately to become King of Israel himself. Much used by the Lord God Almighty to serve the people of the Lord God Almighty ... Here he pauses for a moment in the ongoing reflection of the Psalm, Psalm 16 to turn and cry to the Lord God Almighty and really acknowledge His blessing in his own life , for of all things His counsel in his own life and times. Not only does the Lord God Almighty give David counsel but He has given David a heart that also instructs him in the ways and the paths of the Lord God Almighty. Remember, that David was viewed as a man after the heart of the Lord God Almighty. It is to this that David would appear to alluding in this ...

224

verse? Because David was a man after the heart of the Lord God Almighty, his own heart could and did instruct him in the very ways and the paths of the Lord God Almighty .. David was that close to the very heart of the Lord God Almighty.

The simple reality , is that, we this side of the Cross of Calvary can also be close to the very heart of the Father, the Son and the Holy Spirit; through the Lord

226

Jesus Christ. We too can know and comprehend the very heart of the Father, the Son and the Holy Spirit. It is possible for us to do this in reality through the Lord Jesus Christ and our relationship with Him?

227

Coming after verse 7 we have the very affirmation of faith and belief in the Lord God Almighty by David again. He has ' set ' the Lord God Almighty before himself in his own life. All of which seems to hint at the very reality of a personal choice on the part of David and others to place the Lord God Almighty first in their lives. The Lord God Almighty has the prime place in the life and the very heart of David ... For David there is no other but the Lord God Almighty .. Again, David has nothing to do with the other gods or god that some people worship ...

follow and seek to adhere to? David is a man who follows only the Lord God Almighty; it is He that David chooses to follow , worship and give his loyalty to ... The Lord God Almighty is truly David's God !

231

It is interesting that David says that the Lord God Almighty is at his right hand ... the right hand of the King was the hand of power, authority and even blessing. In the end, David knows where the real power, authority and empowerment he knows , feels and understands in his own life comes from and that is from the Lord God Almighty. This is true, even as David is the King of Israel and the people of the Lord God Almighty, he rules and reigns and has only authority , power and influence because of and through that which is in reality delegated from the Lord God Almighty

234

Himself. David as a man and as a King of the people of the Lord God Almighty knew without question or any argument at all that the real power, authority and influence came from the Lord God Almighty Himself ?

235

The final
clause of verse 8;
' I shall not be
shaken'; is worth
noting as well. In
that, because
David knows the
Lord God
Almighty and has
chosen him , he

knows and sees that he cannot therefore be shaken by anything that happens or comes along in his own life. This is real evidence of a real trust, faith and belief both in the power, authority and influence of the Lord God Almighty ; as well as His ability to help and assist David to not be shaken or wiped out by anything that comes his way.

David knows that the Lord God

has all the power and authority , as well as the ability and desire to keep him both safe and well and to help him remain standing in the Lord God Almighty. This is something which we all need to rediscover and apply to our own lives before the very gaze of the Lord Jesus Christ, the Father, and the Holy Spirit. It is a tremendous thing to be able to remain standing in our faith and belief in the Lord Jesus

Christ. As the Apostle Paul said in the Letter to the Ephesians ' when you have done everything just stand your ground?' Therefore, this Psalm has some real and valid application for us all.

In the end, we too need to know that we do not rule or reign in this world - at - large against the world, the flesh or the Devil in and through our own power and authority! Instead,

242

we only have the ability, the power and the authority to stand and to seek to stand because of that which comes from the Father, the Son of God, and the Holy Spirit. We can stand only because of the Lord God Almighty in us !

244

245

246

247

248

249

250

251

254

255

9.

Finally, in this chapter we will give some consideration

to verses 9 - 11 and see what they have to say to us all? The hope that David has becomes much more real !

(ESV)
"(9)Therefore my heart is glad, and my whole being rejoice; my flesh also dwells secure.

262

(10) For you will not abandon my soul to Sheol, or let your holy one see corruption. (11) You make known

to me the path
of life; in your
presence
there is
fullness of joy;
at your right
hand are
pleasures

264

forevermore."

These three verses are a fitting conclusion to the Psalm, Psalm 16. In many ways, they are in and of themselves caught up with the very reasons why David both cries out to the Lord God Almighty for help and also they describe why he trusts the Lord God as well.

This assurance that David has in the Lord God Almighty affects all of his life.

It affects his whole being as a human being. David is secure and finds his own security in the Lord God Almighty; which is why he wants nothing to do with the other gods and god that some of the people worship.

However, it is not only that David finds his security in the Lord God Almighty but this also causes him to both rejoice and have joy in the Lord God Almighty. It all makes David want to worship ..

268

the Lord God
Almighty he
chooses to follow,
worship and even
rejoice in and
through.

Verse 10
and it's very tone is
different from
verse 9 and what
has gone before in

the very Psalm, Psalm 16? David, the man, the King of Israel, the man after the heart of the Lord God Almighty is also assured that he will not die and be left to the world of the dead, Sheol ?

David has a hope that even in death , the Lord God Almighty will bless him as well. There is a real hint and allusion to the after - life and being with the Lord God Almighty for an eternity in heaven?

271

Admittedly, this hope of an after - life and an assurance of going to heaven is not as full - blown as it is later in the writings of the New Testament but it is still present in these verses. It is interesting that David sees himself as being a 'holy one' and thus the implication is that, because of this inherent holiness he will be able to avoid the corruption of the World of the Dead;

273

namely Sheol? The holiness that David is talking about here would be an imputed holiness because there was no one without the scourge of sin in their own lives in Old Testament times. There was no one who could fully obey the commandments of the Lord God Almighty. Until that is, the very Son of God, the Lord Jesus Christ came to the earth; the spotless lamb of God? In some ways, these verses and their call to be ' holy ones' in the very sight of the Lord God Almighty foreshadow the coming, life , death and resurrection of the Son of God, the Lord Jesus Christ. He was the true ..

'Holy One' who was yet to come on the scene ... How much David understood about the coming of the Lord Jesus Christ; the true 'Holy One' is debatable? Yet, these verses do in reality highlight ...

the very real need
of a ' Holy One ' to
come and be
present amongst
the very people of
the Lord God
Almighty. Because
as good as David
was in being a
man after the heart
of the Lord God; he

was not technically a ' Holy One'; one that is without any sin, spotless and without any blemish of wrong doing or sin in the eyes of the Lord God Almighty.

Verse 11 is a very fitting conclusion to the whole of the

Psalm, Psalm 16. It is a verse of three stages of cause and effect; path of life being made known by the Lord God, presence of the Lord God Almighty and fullness of joy and finally the concept of there being pleasures at the very right hand of the Lord God Almighty forevermore. The hints of an eternity with the Lord God Almighty are now in this verse, verse 11 full - blown and stated very clearly for us all as reader's of this Psalm, Psalm 16 in the Psalter.

Within verse 11, the hope of David in the Lord God Almighty is made very clear. David not only trusts the Lord God

282

Almighty but he also has a very real and realized hope of an eternity with the Lord God Almighty.... David sees this eternity with the Lord God Almighty in a hugely positive light ... It is not an after - thought on

David's part. He fully expects the Lord God Almighty to receive him and for eternity with Him to be a very pleasurable experience for himself. ... 'pleasures forevermore ?'

284

Verse 11 concludes the song of the heart of David to the Lord God Almighty; his God, the One that he follows rather than the other gods and god that some people of the Lord God follow ?

285

In all of this verse 11 could be seen as a very clear statement of why the people of the Lord God Almighty, His chosen people, His treasured possession should not be following other gods or a god other than Him? In this statement against the following of other gods and a god other than the true Lord God Almighty, this verse accords with the rest of the Psalm, Psalm 16 that has gone on before it ? All of which is why it is such a very way and means of concluding this song of the heart, or is a prayer from the very heart of David himself, or is it rather a real and fervent cry for the help of the Lord God Almighty from the man after His own heart David ?

288

However, you want to see and take verse 11 of Psalm 16 , it is in the end a high note of praise of the Lord God Almighty to end this very Psalm, Psalm 16 on?

290

292

294

295

10.

EPILOGUE :

Now we have come to the point of summing up this very book ?

What was seen as a cry to the Lord God Almighty for help in tribulation has become a polemic against foreign gods and

their worship.
David, himself
has chosen to
follow the Lord
God Almighty
and wants
everyone to
follow Him and
yet he himself
300

knows that amongst the very people of the Land and the Lord God Almighty there are people who follow other gods? He is at pains to explain why he himself follows the Lord God Almighty. He presents Him as the true, real and worthwhile Lord God Almighty who should be worshiped and adored by all people; particularly those who are His people, the people of the Land , His treasured people!

As the
Psalm flows
along we see that
David has a very
real hope and
faith and belief
that he himself
has an eternal
future with the

Lord God Almighty. In the end, he knows that he knows that this Lord God Almighty, is the One true God , and the One who holds his future!

This Psalm, Psalm 16 does remain a very heartfelt cry for the Lord God Almighty to help the Psalmist David and His people as well !

However, this very cry from the heart of David the Psalmist is based on the truth of what he knows and understands about the Lord God Almighty. He

is crying out to
the Lord God
Almighty, the Lord
God he knows full
well will help him
and aid him in his
problems as well
as the very people
of the Lord God

who are following after false and untrue gods and a god ... David wants them to come back to their right and true worship of the One true and Living Lord

God Almighty. He wants them to come back and have a real faith and belief in the One true Lord God Almighty , who he himself knows well !

310

This Psalm ends in real praise to the Lord God Almighty, the One true and the Living Lord God Almighty who can be trusted !

311

Therefore while the title of this book does see this Psalm, Psalm 16 as a very real cry out to the Lord God Almighty, it also has so much more to it as well!

It is rather a definitive statement of why have faith, belief and hope in the Lord God Almighty. How much more should we have faith in the Lord Jesus Christ! 313

The
Author :

JOHN C BURT.

JOHN HAS FOLLOWED THE LORD JESUS CHRIST FOR FORTY - THREE YEARS A LIFE FULL OF FUN, ADVENTURE AND LOVE !

318

MY PRAYER IS
THAT YOU ALL
FIND AND ARE
FOUND BY THE
LORD JESUS
CHRIST, THE ONE
GOD, LIVING AND
ALIVE TODAY !!!

319

A PRAYER YOU
MIGHT WANT TO
PRAY IS :
   DEAR LORD
JESUS CHRIST :
   HELP ME TO
LOVE , HONOR
AND OBEY YOU IN
ALL THINGS !
320

HELP ME HOLD
FAST TO MY FAITH
AND MY BELIEF
IN YOU, THE
FATHER, AND THE
HOLY SPIRIT !!!
Amen..... and
AMEN!!!

321

328

329

330

Lightning Source UK Ltd.
Milton Keynes UK
UKRC021223290720
367276UK00014BA/198/J

9 781715 099169